The Man With No Head

The Man With No Head

The Life and Ideas of Douglas Harding
Philosopher, Scientist, Artist, Mystic

Script
Richard Lang

Art
Victor Lunn-Rockliffe

THE SHOLLOND TRUST

THE MAN WITH NO HEAD
Published 2017 by The Shollond Trust.
The Shollond Trust is a UK charity, reg. no. 1059551.

The Shollond Trust, 87B Cazenove Road, London N16 6BB.
www.headless.org

ISBN: 978-1-908774-24-8

The best day of my life
— my rebirthday, so to speak —
was when I found I had no head.

Douglas Harding

what am I?

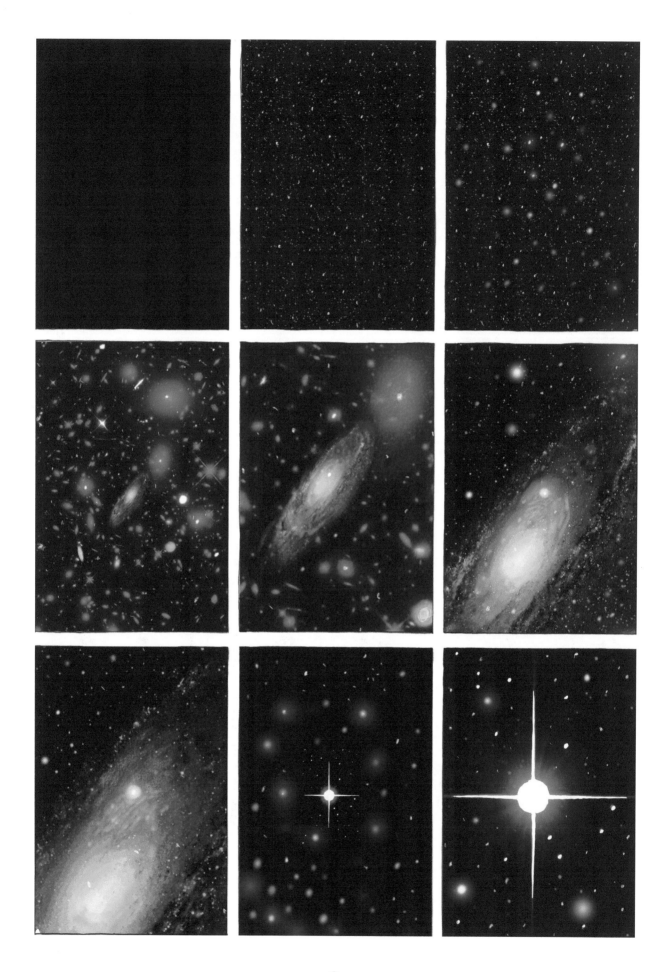

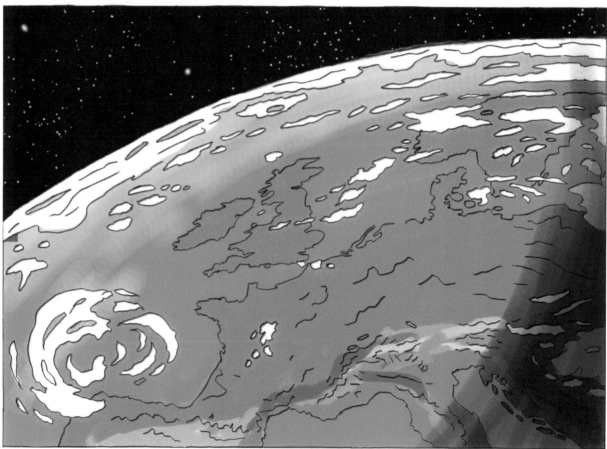

What I am depends
on the range
of the observer.

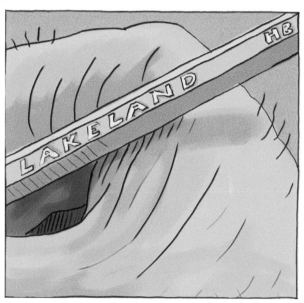

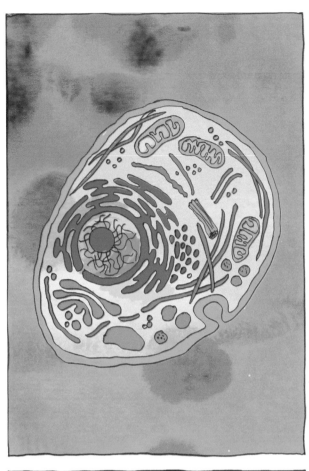
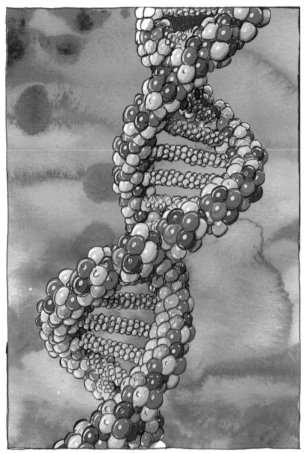

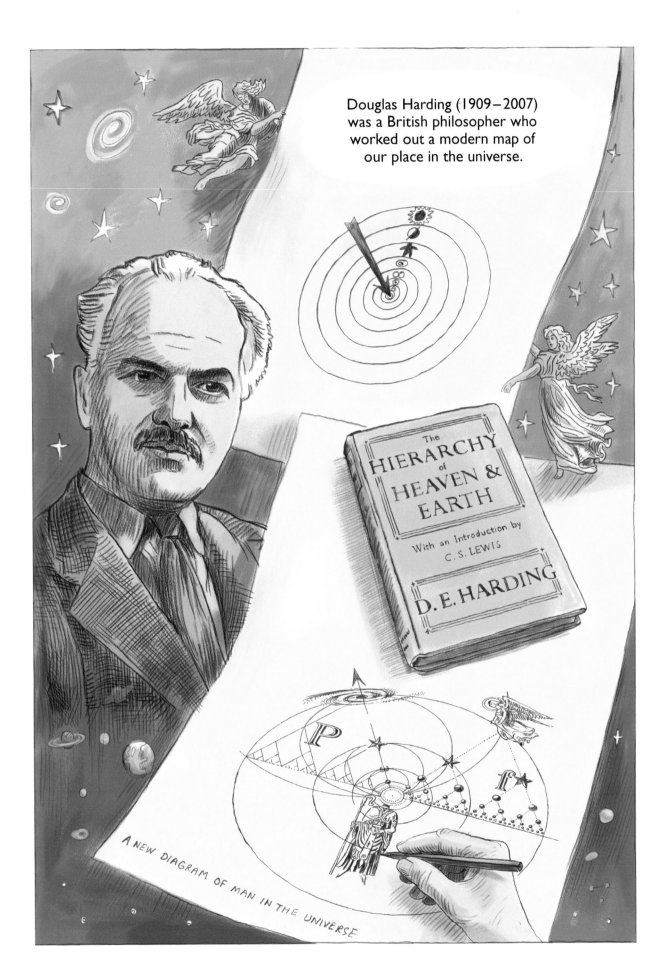

Douglas Harding (1909–2007) was a British philosopher who worked out a modern map of our place in the universe.

12

13

*"This is not a literary gambit,
a witticism designed to arouse interest
at any cost.
I mean it in all seriousness:
I have no head."*

What led Douglas Harding
to make this astonishing claim?
What did he mean?

What was Harding's modern map
of our place in the universe,
his 'Hierarchy of Heaven and Earth'?

How did Harding
eventually share his Vision
with thousands of people?

Douglas Harding was born on February 12, 1909 in Lowestoft, Suffolk, on the east coast of England, overlooking the North Sea.

Lowestoft is the most easterly town in England.

It was a mostly High Victorian town uncertain whether its business was netting fish or summer visitors.

19

In 1916 German battleships shelled Lowestoft.

THE·COSY·CORNER

Mr. Harding, bring your family into the basement of the cinema where they'll be safe.

Thank you, but no. We're going to stay at home and pray.

Come on everyone, we're going to put ourselves in the Lord's hands.

Douglas was 7.

21

Can I go round to John's house?

We keep separate from the evil world, Douglas, so you can't play with non-Brethren children.

Go for a walk on your own by the sea, son.

Precious jewels!

It's my secret magic trick.

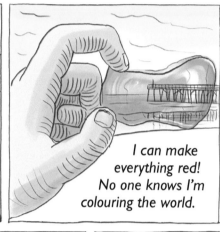
I can make everything red! No one knows I'm colouring the world.

What's that in your pocket, Douglas?

My sapphires and emeralds, Miss Chipperfield.

Dirty bits of glass. Throw them in the bin!

No! I can paint the world with them.

Nonsense! You can't do that. You don't have magic powers. Grow up!

You're wrong. I do have magic powers.

We will now learn the names of the capes and bays of Great Britain.

I refuse to learn anything from you ever again.

This is Billy's collection of pressed leaves.

I want to do that.

Douglas began collecting the next day.

Horse chestnut. I haven't got one of those.

Within a week he had the best collection in class.

Very good, Douglas!

Ammonites! Belemnites!

He has my energy.

A monarch. Very rare!

Douglas always has a project on. And he never does anything by half.

The experience of organising his collections would prove useful, years later, when Douglas took on the huge task of writing *The Hierarchy of Heaven & Earth*.

When Douglas was 10 he was playing tennis with his cousin.

Suddenly Eileen stopped.

You've got a red nose!

Douglas rushed indoors.

She's right. It's horribly red.

This will disguise the colour.

Ashamed of his face, Douglas went to school by the backstreets to avoid meeting anyone he knew.

At school.

Douglas has toothpaste on his nose!

Look!

Ha, ha!

No I don't!

Douglas now hated his face. Later, as an adult, his need to free himself of his morbid self-consciousness would make his search for his 'Original Face' – his True Self – more than just an intellectual exercise.

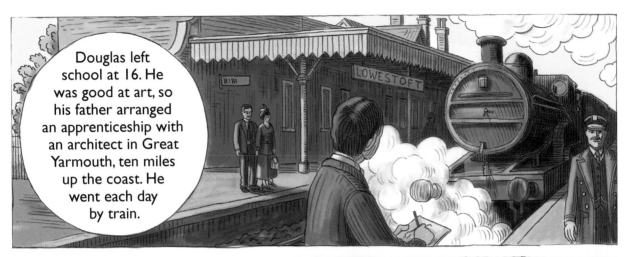

Douglas left school at 16. He was good at art, so his father arranged an apprenticeship with an architect in Great Yarmouth, ten miles up the coast. He went each day by train.

LOWESTOFT

Douglas realised he wasn't learning much. To pass the architectural exams he began secretly revising in the Brethren meetings.

The Parthenon was a Doric temple with Ionic architectural features.

He's so holy.

Douglas passed the Intermediate exams of the Royal Institute of British Architecture.

Amazing! I came top in the British Empire!

I'm 19 and at University College in London!

1928

Later, Douglas' father blamed this move to London for leading his son away from all he held dear...

26

Edgar heard about the essay.

I'm going to London to stop Douglas from making a huge mistake.

My son, I'd rather you'd committed a murder than leave the Brethren.

I'm not changing my mind.

You will burn in Hell forever!

Douglas was thrown out of his lodgings. Twice! His first landlady was a Plymouth Sister.

I'm sorry, the Brethren won't let me rent a room to you anymore.

I understand, Mrs. Fox. They think I'm evil.

By chance his next landlady turned out to be a Plymouth Sister as well!

I'm rather enjoying my reputation!

I've just found out who you are. You're in league with the devil!

Douglas' parents cut off all contact. No longer restricted by the Brethren's rules, Douglas now felt free to explore life...

This is the first film I've ever seen.

All Quiet on the Western Front

It's as powerful as reading Dickens for the first time.

Plainsong! I feel lifted out of myself.

Society must change!

Hey you, stop!

Communist hooligan!

After qualifying as an architect, Douglas found a job in the City.

I'll pay you £3 per week.

Yes, Mr. Low.

But Douglas' main interest was not architecture.

Who is this person called Douglas?

What is life about?

Why are we here?

What am I?

Douglas visited the library in his lunch hour.

According to science I'm not simply human.

I have layers.

HUMAN CELLS

At close range

I'm a society of primitive animals,

CELL CLUB

a walking cell-city.

What is the relationship between me and my cells?

Each cell lives its life unaware of me. Yet all my cells working together are me. I'm a king who is his subjects!

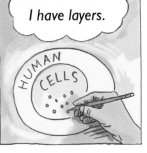

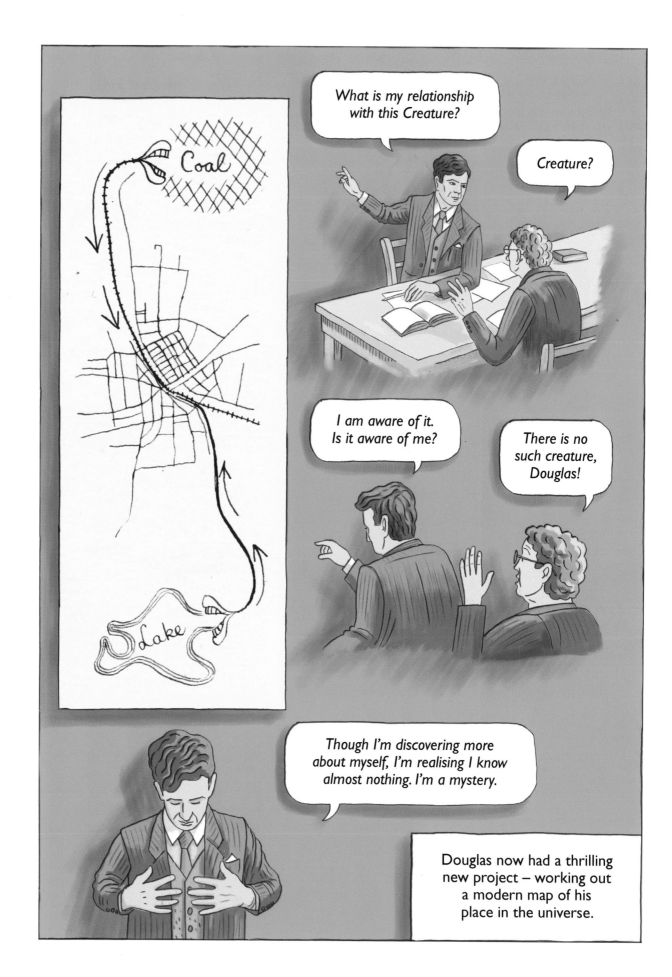

Douglas, I disagree with you. You are your body. You stop at your skin. You are not these artificial 'limbs' and 'organs'.

YOU

If you had false teeth, would they be part of your body?

No!

Why?

Because they are dead.

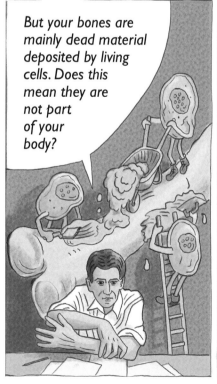

But your bones are mainly dead material deposited by living cells. Does this mean they are not part of your body?

No, because they are not loose like my false teeth.

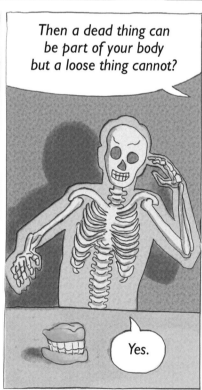

Then a dead thing can be part of your body but a loose thing cannot?

Yes.

34

Douglas was working out that he was built to a hierarchical pattern.

The parts of one level combine to form the whole of the next level.

And I join with all people and all our artefacts to form an even higher being — the Creature, which I call 'Humanity'.

All my cells join together to form me.

THE MEANING AND BEAUTY OF THE ARTIFICIAL

My molecules combine into cells.

My atoms combine into molecules.

Each of my atoms is a society of particles.

HUMANITY

CELL CLUB

PERSON

CELL

ATOM CLUB

MOLECULE

ATOM

PARTICLE

Though Douglas was aware that through tools we grow, he was also aware of their danger. Germany was re-arming.

We must uncover the root causes of conflict so we can beat our swords into ploughshares.

GERMANY CONTINUES TO REARM

Douglas also had ambitions to be a novelist. He wrote short stories.

The Nightmare Nose

The Red Fro[...]

The Stink

Mourning For Grandfather

The Plymouth Brother

Meanwhile he met Chloe. They had a brief relationship. Chloe became pregnant.

Will you marry me?

I don't want to marry

but I want to avoid a scandal. So I'm moving to Spain.

Douglas then met Beryl. They were both interested in politics.

Communism addresses social injustice.

WORKERS INTERNATIONAL LEAGUE

THE CP COMMUNIST PARTY OF GREAT BRITAIN

They married in December 1935.

In 1936 they visited Russia to observe Communism in action.

It was during Stalin's Purge. Douglas' growing doubts about the Soviet panacea turned to horror.

The fear and poverty everywhere is terrible.

Beryl became pregnant. At the same time Douglas got a job as an architect in Calcutta.

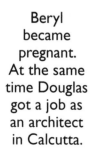

The pay is better.

With war coming, it will be safer to raise a family there.

In 1937 they sailed for India.

Soon after they arrived Julian was born. Then the next year, Simon.

Douglas managed a large architectural team.

We must build this differently or it will fall down.

Yes, sir.

Douglas was determined to make his mark on the world.

He took many photographs, winning an award.

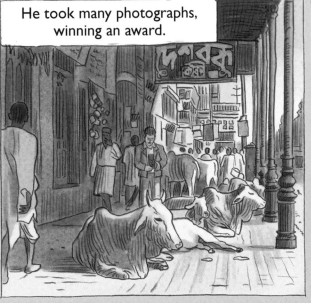

He became a cartoonist and had an exhibition.

And he wrote a detective novel. A man is found dead. He's faceless – his face had been destroyed by a shotgun.

It was a strange preview of what would happen to Douglas a few years later…

In 1940, because of the War, Beryl left India with the children to take refuge in America.

The next year Douglas joined the Army. He was 32.

My centre seems hidden, inaccessible.

The closer an observer gets to me, the less he finds.

What am I at zero distance?

It makes sense that at centre I am 'nothing',

but how can I verify that?

In 1943 Douglas found what he was looking for…

As a member of the Imperial Library, Douglas had access to many books.

He discovered a self-portrait by the physicist Ernst Mach.

How unusual! Normally when drawing yourself you use a mirror.

You draw what you look like from a few feet.

But Mach hasn't used a mirror. This is himself from zero distance.

My goodness! I'm headless too!

I am seeing what I am at centre. I am capacity for the world!

I'm not in my body, my body is in me.

I'm not moving, the street is moving.

I have your faces instead of mine. I am you.

Douglas felt deep peace, a quiet joy,
and the sensation of having dropped an intolerable burden.

48

49

Soon after seeing he had no head, Douglas experienced a turning point.

The Saturday Club
Calcutta

My life must now be about this vision.

To present my discoveries to the world, I must educate myself.

I don't know enough philosophy, science, history, psychology…

No more photographs, cartoons, novels… I must get down to serious work.

He developed a card index system.

Organising all these ideas is the key.

Shortly before the end of the War Douglas was posted back to England.

He was re-united with his family.

After a year he left the Army – having been promoted to Deputy Commander, Royal Engineers. The family settled in Ipswich.

Beryl, I want to take a year to finish my book before returning to architecture. I saved money in India, so we can manage.

Of course. You must get this off your chest.

Beryl got a job teaching.

Douglas also taught — two classes a week, on philosophy and comparative religion.

The rest of the time he worked on his book.

Dad...

I'm busy.

Come on, let's take Plato for a walk.

Putting the past behind them, his parents resumed contact.

Beryl says you are writing a book.

Yes. It keeps growing!

He corresponded with Chloe about their daughter, Lydia.

'What am I?' That is my question.

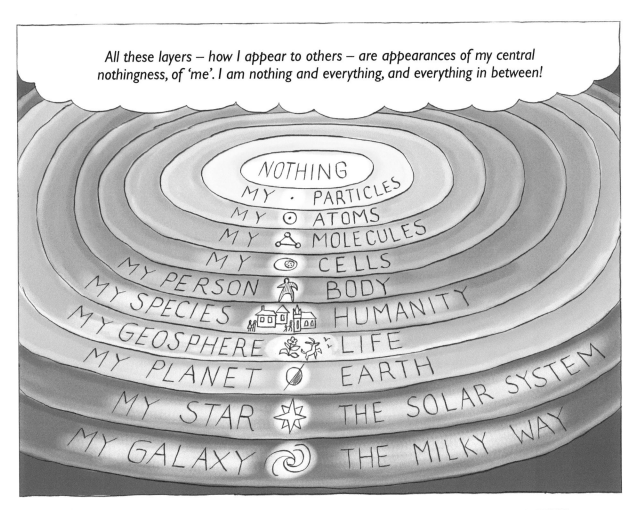

Though I am nothing for myself at centre, for those people over there I appear as a man.

From the Moon
I am no longer
human. I have a
planetary body.

But although other people see a person here,

I don't. My body vanishes into this central void. I, this person, am absent. I am empty for others.

And although from those stars I am a star,

I see no star here. Being this star means being room for other stars.

I grow and shrink depending on how far I look. One moment I'm this person, yet room for other people; the next moment I'm this planet or star, yet room for other planets, other stars.

But the ground beneath my feet is not only planetary and solar, it is also galactic!

Understanding these truths is not enough. They have to be lived to become real.

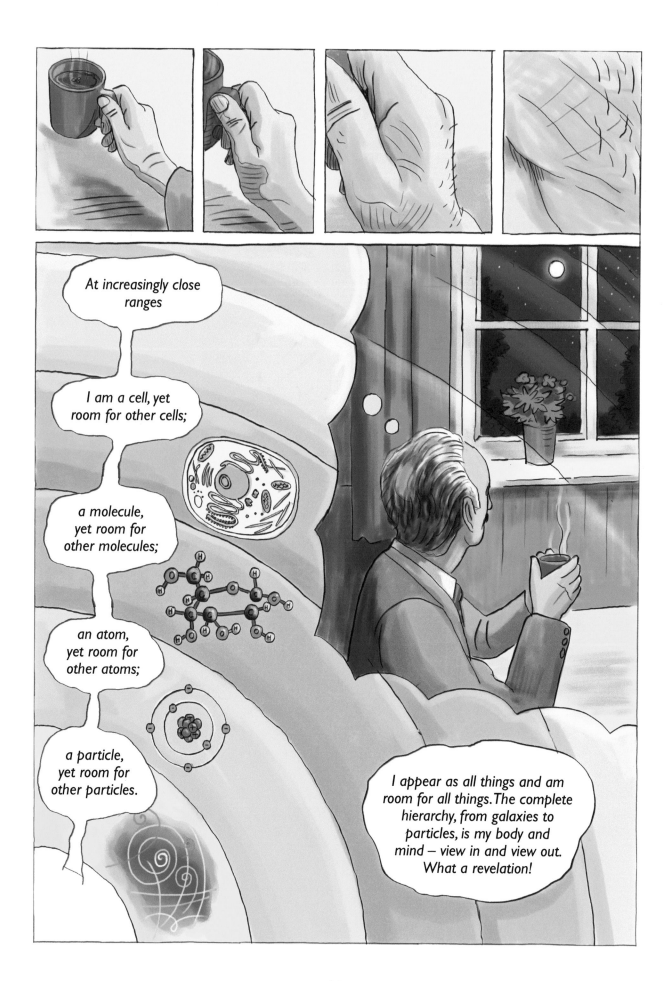

Being aware of this headless Capacity changes how I see everything. The many-layered universe is in me. I am infinitely rich!

I gain insight into every being.
Each is small for others but immense
for itself. Each contains all.

Where are my thoughts?

My thoughts are not imprisoned in a central container here but merge with the world.

Seeing no
boundary
to myself,
I find
myself
identifying
with others.

Placing
myself at
their centres,
I become
others,
feeling for
and as
them.

PAAAP

I can also feel my way into inanimate things.

In the taut rope I feel the pull.

I hover in the clouds,

shine as the sun,

look down from the stars.

Being nothing at centre means I can place myself at other centres.

The ability to shift centre is the basis of love.

This was a period of profound study and reflection, a maturing of his vision.

This humble Centre is the locus of the Whole. Tremendous fact!

Whatever I look at, I become.

Lifting this stone, I am there.

My life is the life that others live in me.

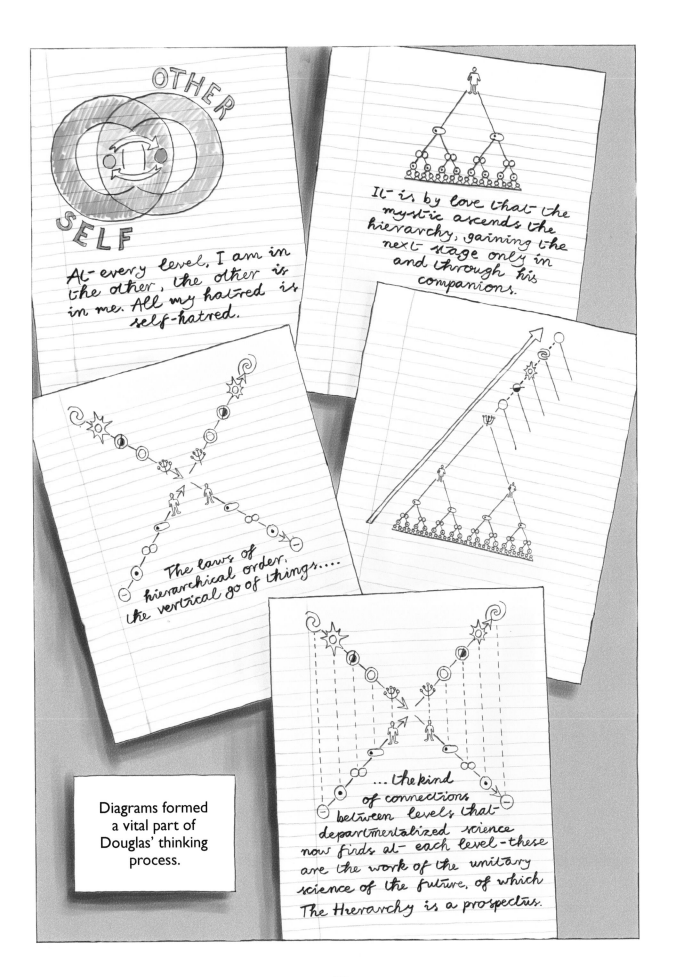

OTHER

SELF

At every level, I am in the other, the other is in me. All my hatred is self-hatred.

It is by love that the mystic ascends the hierarchy, gaining the next stage only in and through his companions.

The laws of hierarchical order, the vertical go of things....

...the kind of connections between levels that departmentalized science now finds at each level — these are the work of the unitary science of the future, of which The Hierarchy is a prospectus.

Diagrams formed a vital part of Douglas' thinking process.

In the summer of 1948 Douglas finished the first draft of *The Hierarchy of Heaven & Earth*.

By the spring of 1949 he had typed up the first half. He sent this to Cyprian Blagden, a friend at the publisher Longman.

21 July 1949

Dear Douglas,
The Hierarchy is very impressive, but I'm afraid it's unpublishable. You would do better to stop and go back to architecture.

Cyprian replied.

You look pale, Douglas.

Cyprian thinks I'm wasting my time. I'm going out for a walk.

This is a big shock.

I have to face the fact that my life's work may never see the light of day.

But I don't care if no one reads it. I'm going to finish the job, come what may.

CHAPTER XVI
TIME MOTION AND STRUCTURE

Only occasionally did Douglas take time off from his book.

Julian, we're going to visit Grandma and Grandpa in Lowestoft.

I want to go on my new bike.

I need a bike. The cheapest you've got.

This is second-hand, but it's a boneshaker!

Perfect!

Where's your father?

Hello, Grandpa. Dad is a bit slow...

What happened?

Julian left me behind.

I'm exhausted and annoyed. It was a mad idea to cycle. We're going home by train.

Back home.

Beryl, I still have more work to do on my book.

Take as long as you need, Douglas.

75

Writing *The Hierarchy* took Douglas on a tremendous adventure.

Where do my ideas come from?

The Centre guides me to a book.

An idea or image appears from this unknowable Depth within me.

Often I do not understand a diagram at first.

But as I work with it — as it works with me — its meaning unfolds. It teaches me.

The living universe is revealing its amazing structure in me.

All I have discovered is only a fraction of the truth. The mystery extends in every direction to infinity.

As well as the countless miracles we comprise, there is that supreme irregularity — the fact that anything exists at all. There is not just Nothing. How adroit of It to happen!

My finest, most thrilling discovery is that, because all my roots are in the Undiscoverable, I also am undiscoverable.

Though writing *The Hierarchy* was a profound mystical experience for Douglas, his realisations took time to affect his personality.

I've been invited to teach a weekly class on Logic at the WEA in Colchester.

That's good news.

WORKERS' EDUCATIONAL ASSOCIATION

Welcome, Mr. Harding.

We've heard good reports of you.

Oh no! I'm beginning to feel self-conscious. I can hardly look at anyone.

I'm feeling intensely aware of my face.

I'm shaking all over. I'm a mass of nerves.

Thank you, Mr. Harding. See you next week.

That was difficult. I felt painfully self-conscious again, under inspection, trapped and afraid. I couldn't look in anyone's eyes.

Finishing the typescript in September 1950, Douglas immediately began a shorter version to offer to publishers.

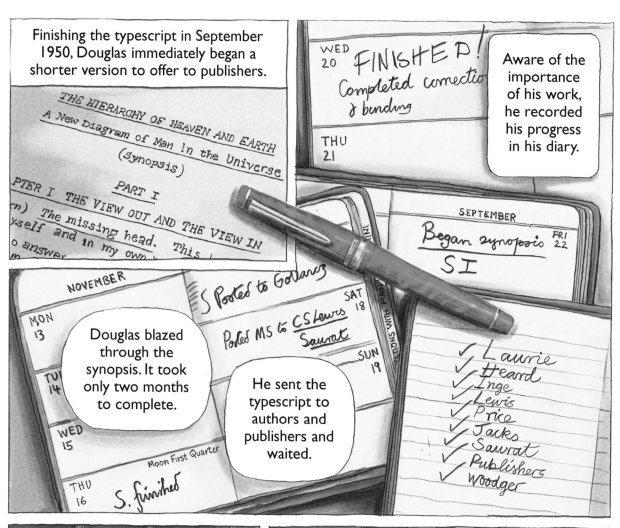

THE HIERARCHY OF HEAVEN AND EARTH
A New Diagram of Man in the Universe
(synopsis)

PART I

PTER I   THE VIEW OUT AND THE VIEW IN

WED 20 FINISHED!
Completed correctio
& binding

THU 21

Aware of the importance of his work, he recorded his progress in his diary.

SEPTEMBER
Began synopsis   FRI 22
S I

✓ Laurie
✓ Heard
✓ Inge
✓ Lewis
✓ Price
✓ Jacks
✓ Saurat
✓ Publishers
✓ Woodger

NOVEMBER

MON 13

Posted to Gollancz
Posted MS to C S Lewis   SAT 18
Saurat
SUN 19

TUE 14

WED 15

Moon First Quarter

THU 16   S. finished

Douglas blazed through the synopsis. It took only two months to complete.

He sent the typescript to authors and publishers and waited.

Meanwhile Beryl was sworn in as a magistrate.

Douglas began looking for a job.

Air Ministry
The Gas Board
Ministry of Works
Architects

Good news, Beryl. My old friend Eric Sandon wants me to join him as partner in his architectural firm!

Douglas finished a second detective novel he had begun in India.

The Melwold Mystery

MARCH
MON 26
TUE 27
WED 28   CSL letter!

Then he received a letter from C. S. Lewis...

Magdalen etc
Easter Day 1951

Hang it all, you've made me drunk, roaring drunk

you have written a work of the highest genius.

At last someone understands me!

Lewis invited Douglas to Oxford.

4th June
Let me have a card by return, and I'll book a room.
Yours,
C. S. Lewis

*Your book is a completely fresh look at our place in the universe — in the **living** universe! It's revolutionary.*

Douglas' mother died whilst he was visiting Lewis. She had been ill.

A few months later.

Lewis has written a preface. He's put his neck out for me. I'll always be grateful to him.

Published by Faber & Faber in 1952.

The
HIERARCHY
of
HEAVEN &
EARTH

With an Introduction by
C. S. LEWIS

D. E. HARDING

A book of immense originality.

E. Fuller, Episcopal Church News.

Ten year job finished!

Douglas quickly built up a successful architectural practice with Eric Sandon.

SANDON & HARDING ARCHITECTS

He designed and built a house. 'Shollond Hill' was in the village of Nacton, near Ipswich.

1956

It's very modern, Dad.

Meanwhile, Douglas continued his life's work. He wrote a drama, a presentation of some of the ideas in *The Hierarchy of Heaven & Earth*.

VISIBLE GODS

Visible Gods is an imagined conversation between Socrates and several modern thinkers.

You agree that the universe is a many-levelled living whole; that the stars are 'visible gods'.

You've twisted our words, Socrates.

I've only developed your argument to its conclusion!

The universe is not living! Only tiny bits of it are alive.

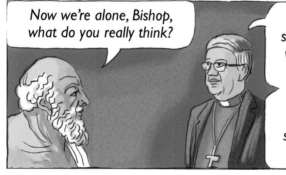

Now we're alone, Bishop, what do you really think?

My dear Socrates, you show us the living universe with our own science, but we refuse to accept it.

We 'know' the universe is dead and anyone who says otherwise we dismiss as poet or madman.

Ahead of its time, Douglas' worldview was generally ignored.

September, 1957

My sister phoned. Father has died.

Edgar was a good Plymouth Brother who accepted with grace the wickedness of his son.

Everyone is welcome back in the hall for tea, except Mr. Harding.

They can't burn me at the stake, so they do the next worst thing in England — they refuse me tea!

Douglas met his sister Freda to sort out their father's will, in a lay-by on the A12.

I refuse to meet inside, under the same roof as you, because you left our dear father's faith.

Later, back home.

Do you miss your father?

Yes, Beryl, I loved him enormously. His complete dedication to the truth as he saw it inspires me. How I hurt him by leaving the Brethren.

I'm making money, I've taken care of my family, I've no more worldly ambitions.

But I'm nearly 50. I'm treading water. What's the next step in my life's work?

It was as if the universe answered Douglas' question.

The *Saturday Evening Post* requested an article.

My chance to reach a huge audience.

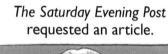
The Universe Revalued
Every age has it's
world-picture.

The acclaimed photographer, Tom Blau, took Douglas' portrait for *The Post*.

Douglas' article attracted attention.

The Saturday Evening POST March 4 1961 15¢

ACADEMY OF ACHIEVEMENT
Monterey, California, June 26, 1961
Dear Mr. Harding: The Academy invites you to the banquet as a guest of honor.

But though he was beginning to be noticed, Douglas remained his own man.

Edward Teller, 'father of the hydrogen bomb'.

The Russians are overtaking us technically. We must bomb them now before it's too late.

It's disgraceful.

Yes, Roethke, I won't stand and applaud that!

Communist!

Thank you! We want to shake your hand.

Douglas discovered Zen.

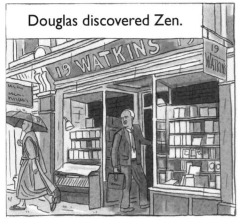

Hui-neng saw what I see – this faceless space.

Show me the truth, Hui-neng.

Look at your Original Face, Ming – the Face you had before you were born.

Zen speaks my language. At last I am in the company of headless Seers.

On Having No Head a contribution to zen in the west

If I set my headless revelation where I walked in the Himalayas, it will grab the reader's attention…

Perhaps Buddhists will value headlessness.

I want to register for The Buddhist Society Summer School.

Douglas became a familiar face at the Summer School.

Harding's book shows fresh insight into Zen.

Yes, he appeals to direct experience.

On Having No Head became a modern spiritual classic.

Douglas also read *Talks with Ramana Maharshi*.

Ramana is right, the Self is obvious. Anyone can see this Space.

I feel his presence helping me abide steadily in the Self. No more wavering.

Douglas, Helen is our new secretary.

Douglas, may I read your book?

Of course, Helen.

1964

A few days later.

I think I see what you mean. I'm Space for the world.

Yes, you do see it.

Seeing had a dramatic effect on Helen.

Suddenly she is beating everyone!

Being out of the way, I play better!

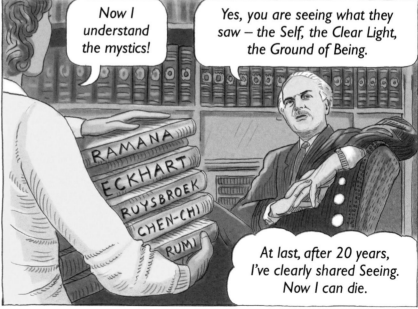

Now I understand the mystics!

Yes, you are seeing what they saw – the Self, the Clear Light, the Ground of Being.

RAMANA
ECKHART
RUYSBROEK
CHEN-CHI
RUMI

At last, after 20 years, I've clearly shared Seeing. Now I can die.

Douglas began sharing Seeing with more people, but his family were not interested.

Two people saw their No-face at my talk!

They glimpsed something, Father, but they're not Enlightened.

Nor are you, Douglas.

Douglas met his daughter Lydia for the first time.

He's not interested in me, only in Seeing.

Douglas built a second house across the lane.

'Under Shollond' will be a place for Seeing friends.

In December 1965 Douglas revisited India.

Ramana Ashram

One reason for the trip was to distance himself from Helen.

You're very special, Douglas.

I'm fond of you, Helen, but we're just friends. You must separate me from Seeing.

Douglas met the saint Anandamayi Ma.

Ma has asked me to give you her shawl and says, "I am you, I am you."

February, 1966

Welcome back to the office, Douglas. I have some news. I'm engaged to Helen!

Congratulations, Eric.

Helen now distanced herself from Douglas.

I feel close to mystics of all traditions. They value this Nothingness which the world ignores.

Douglas was commissioned to write a book.

We would like you to write about the world's chief religions.

What an opportunity!

RELIGIONS OF THE WORLD
HI

HINDUISM
The story of the great religions begins in India.

There is but One. He who divides the One wanders from death to death.

The UPANISHADS

Liberation is realising you are the One. Only the One is truly free.

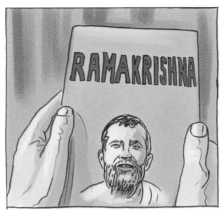

I see God more clearly than I see you.

I can only glimpse faces, but I see my No-face perfectly. At my centre alone is that which is truly visible and real — the One, the Alone.

Seeing the truth through the eyes of great sages is deeply inspiring.

Douglas was teaching comparative religion once a week.

You are enthusiastic about each religion!

Each celebrates Reality in a unique way.

BUDDHIS

The Buddha gave important advice to the monk Ananda.

BUDDHISM VOID

Be your own authority. Do not depend on others.

Looking for yourself at what you are is more important than relying on any text or teacher.

Aren't you Douglas Harding?

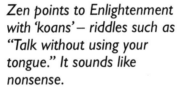

Yes. I'm reading up on Zen for my book on world religions.

Zen points to Enlightenment with 'koans' – riddles such as "Talk without using your tongue." It sounds like nonsense.

Look! Notice you can't see your tongue. Your words come from Emptiness, from Silence.

Don't I have to purify myself before I can see my Buddha-nature?

No! As Zen Master Ummon said, "Get Enlightened first, deal with your bad karma afterwards!"

But I have many faults.

We all do but they are peripheral, not central. They do not obscure your True Self.

Sounds too easy!

Seeing your Buddha-nature is easy. Living from it is the challenge.

Surely I must cultivate special qualities.

Water the Root and the flower will take care of itself.

I'll have to think about that.

Don't think, look!

Thou art the soul of my soul.
Solomon ibn Gabirol

Though Judaism places God 'out there', commanding His people to walk in justice, yet it also finds Him 'in here'.

Harding here. Can I speak with my editor?

He's not in? I've called several times now.

You suggest I call again tomorrow…

Frustrating!

Others gain authority over you if you possess a will distinct from God's will.

Rabbi Nachman

When things don't go my way I feel powerless, at the mercy of others. Life isn't fair.

*But not talking to my editor must be what God deems just and fair for me. It's not what **I** want but what **the One** wants.*

*Yet I am the One here, so all flows from me and is my will. What happens is therefore what **I** really want. There is no one outside my Self to oppose my will.*

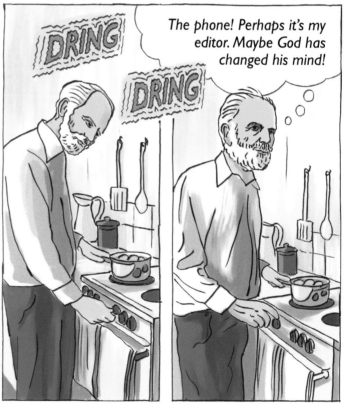

DRING

DRING

The phone! Perhaps it's my editor. Maybe God has changed his mind!

92

Yes? Your name is Martyn. You've just discovered headlessness?

I'll be in London next week. Let's meet up.

I used to come to Westminster Cathedral when I was a young man.

When Jesus said, "I and my Father are one", he was seeing he was God, just as we are seeing that reality now.

But when you say you are God, you don't mean Douglas is God, do you?

No! And I'm sure Jesus did not mean that he, the man, was God.

Jesus was referring to his Reality, not to his appearance. I have an unorthodox view of Jesus.

Jesus also spoke about love: "Love your neighbour as yourself."

Because he saw that his neighbour was himself.

When I see I am empty here,

I die to myself and am reborn as you.

Vanishing in your favour, I become you. This is "giving your life for your friend".

You have a deep love of Christianity.

It's because of my father. His love for Jesus inspired me as a child. Seeing who I am has re-connected me to something very deep inside me.

Thank you for showing me the Truth.

Come and visit. You will meet others who are valuing this Way.

Rumi was a Sufi, an Islamic mystic. He was a great poet

and a whirling dervish.

God is nearer to a man than his jugular vein.
The Koran

Around my still centre the earth and heavens revolve.

I am non-existent, I have given myself up. I am nothing, He is all. There is no being but God's.

The Master has surrendered to the Beloved.

Like Rumi, I am still. The world dances in me.

Saying 'yes' to this Openness is surrendering to Reality.

Seeing I am empty of myself is seeing I am replaced by God.

I have no existence apart from God. God alone is aware. God alone is.

Religions Of The World was published in 1966 and used in schools.

I've read your new book. At the end you reconcile religion and science.

What science tells me about myself — body and mind, at all levels — is a religious revelation.

Being at your physical centre here, you are also at the living heart of each religion.

Each religion highlights an important aspect of Reality — of **your** Reality.

HINDUISM — Oneness
BUDDHISM — Mindfulness
JUDAISM — Justice
CHRISTIANITY — Self-giving love
ISLAM — Surrender

The world's great religions are a living whole. They are branches of one tree.

They are different but complementary voices, spoken by the One who is beyond all words, all images, yet is nearer to you than your breath.

You seem to speak from experience, not just from ideas. How can we experience the One?

Notice you cannot see your face. You are looking out of what Zen calls your 'Original Face'. That formless space is who you really are.

How simple! And true!

May 1st, 1966

Retiring at 57, Douglas! Enjoy your freedom!

Now I can spend even more time on my life's work.

Douglas and Beryl were leading increasingly separate lives.

I have visitors this weekend.

I don't want to meet them, Douglas. I'm not interested in Seeing.

THE DIVIDED SELF R.D. LAING

A Seeing community emerged as Douglas experimented with new ways of sharing.

I don't see who I am.

This shawl from India may help you.

What do you see inside it?

Nothing. Except the world!

You've got it!

Douglas, what's this book about?

It's something I had to work out, but you don't need to read it. Just look there.

The HIERARCHY of HEAVEN & EARTH
with an Introduction by C. S. LEWIS
D. E. HARDING

Nowadays I won't accept people can't See. Of course, valuing it is another thing.

Chiao's Dream

Douglas spoke to a local club for young wives.

I understand what you mean, Douglas.

I can see that, Anne. Come and visit us at Under Shollond.

Douglas explored the psychological implications of Seeing.

Berne's ideas inspired Douglas.

Underlying all psychological games is one master game — pretending you are living from behind a face.

Imagining a face here, I'm putting on an act. I'm playing the Face Game.

This makes us feel separate from others, isolated and alone.

It's the game that I'm behind my face here and you're behind yours there.

Seeing I am faceless is dropping that act, that pretence.

I re-discover the real 'me', which is capacity for you!

Not playing the Face Game leads to true intimacy!

Douglas sent his article to Berne in San Francisco.

"Enlightenment is ceasing to play the game of being a person." We'll publish it.

April, 1967

THE FACE GAME
TRANSACTIONAL ANALYSIS APPLIED TO ZEN
D. E. Harding

The Buddhist Society Summer School	Douglas was making more friends and giving more talks.

How different from all those years on my own.

Nottingham

Doncaster

Bristol

In York Douglas met Mike Heron of The Incredible String Band.

Welcome!

You're right!

In this basement flat is a man with no head!

Why call your song 'Douglas **Traherne** Harding'?

I've used some of Traherne's words in the lyrics.

THOMAS TRAHERNE
1637–1674

CENTURIES

For Mike, with love Dad

Douglas, we're performing at the Albert Hall. Please come.

I would love to.

June 29, 1968

When I was born I had no head.

My eye was single and my body was filled with light.

And the light that I was, was the light that I saw by.

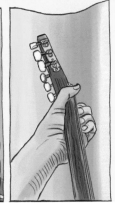

Dear Douglas,
  Back stage at concerts all over, I keep meeting bright beings who have seen you talk or be, or have met you in the pages of your lovely book. It reminds me what a warm affection I hold for you.
Yours in love,
Mike Heron

Are you face-to-face or space-to-face with others?

October, 1968.
A local girls' school.

I heard you speak at my school. I am terribly self-conscious. I feel suicidal. I need help.

Let's meet in the school car park.

I hate my face. I want plastic surgery.

I used to be painfully self-conscious like you.

That has completely gone because now I see **where** my face is. It's out there in others and in the mirror, not here.

You are built open.

Your face is not your problem. It belongs to others.

A year later.

Dear Douglas Harding,

Everything you said made a deep and lasting impression on me and changed my attitude both towards myself and towards other people radically and immediately.

102

Douglas was becoming
better known in the
Buddhist world.

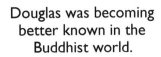

*Welcome to Under
Shollond, Alan.*

*Here's
a copy of
my book,
Douglas.*

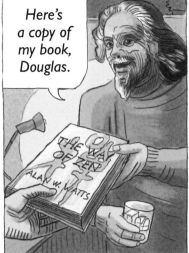

*I want to
understand
headlessness.*

*It's not
a matter of
understanding
but of
seeing.*

The next morning.

*I had a dream. Everyone's head
was replaced by light — **the** Light.*

ON HAVING
NO HEAD

*No, Alan! Others
keep their heads. Only
you, the 1st Person,
are headless.*

*I'm meeting Eric Berne
in San Francisco.*

*Come and give a talk
on my houseboat
in Sausalito.*

As the Heart Sutra says, "Here
form is void and void is form."

June, 1969

Welcome to my home, Douglas.

There's no dividing line. I am you.

The American Zen teacher Kapleau visited.

Under Shollond is the spiritual centre of England!

1970. Kapleau invited Douglas to his Zen Center in America.

A warm welcome to Douglas. He sees his Original Face.

When Douglas returned two years later, things were different.

You won't See if you sit with closed eyes, refusing to do the experiments!

You've heard Douglas. Now one of you come up here and test his Enlightenment!

How does headlessness help when I pull your nose?

What nonsense!

You're preventing me from sharing. I'm being bullied.

I am!

You're cross with me, Douglas.

You passed the test.

I'm not here to be tested. I'm not here to play these silly games.

The simplicity and availability of Seeing threatens his hierarchy and his position at the top.

1971. Douglas visited North America with a young friend.

*Colin, we have a weekend workshop in Toronto. Rather than just **talk** at people, we need to **do things** with them.*

Welcome to 'The Claremont Experiment'.

Do people need to bring anything to the workshop?

A shawl or a towel.

Colin will initiate you into 'Towelism'!

Arrange your towel like this.

Does it frame your face or the world?

It's like a tunnel!

Douglas had an idea during the night.

I'll cut the end off this rubbish bag.

Colin, wake up.

This makes it obvious we are face-to-No-face.

You can't miss it! I am you.

Now Douglas moved away from just talking to including 'experiments'.

Back in England.

Carole and I find that trading faces is the basis of love.

Yes. I'm disappearing in favour of Anne now.

Seeing how effective the experiments were, Douglas rapidly developed his presentation style.

The point is to **experience** *your True Self, not just think about it.*

Point out — you see things.

Point in — no thing!

Point both ways — this Space isn't just empty, it's also full.

You're looking through two holes there.

Put them on. Now you're looking through one hole — your boundless Single Eye!

Turn round. Are you moving or is the world moving?

With eyes closed, how big are you? What shape? How old?

Is your face above your shoulders or in the mirror?

Thank God I'm not like that!

Time and the Timeless

There the moving hands mark out the passage of time. Time and change go together.

Here is no movement, no change, no time. We look into time from the Timeless.

Douglas also developed experiments for groups.

The Unclassifiable Experiment

I'm going to stick a dot on your forehead without you seeing its colour.

The rules are — no talking, no looking in a mirror and no touching the dot.

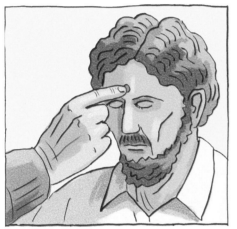

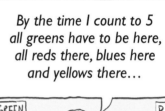

By the time I count to 5 all greens have to be here, all reds there, blues here and yellows there…

GREEN

RED

1, 2, 3, 4, 5. You have to move! Go!

GREEN ! !? !? RED

? ? ! ? ?

108

I moved because you told us to. And if I hadn't moved I wouldn't have learned anything.

Staying still would mean no game, and if there's no game, there's no fun.

We must participate if we want to learn and have adventures — not just in this game but in life as well.

I'm colour-blind. I realise I put you in the wrong group.

I trusted you!

Others tell us who we are. Though they are not completely reliable, functioning in society involves trusting others.

I felt left out until someone welcomed me into a group.

We all have a profound need to belong.

I don't like being labelled. It's restricting.

Our resistance is understandable!

Our identity is two-sided. Publicly I'm classifiable. You identify me as a person – as Douglas. I rely on your feedback to know myself.

But privately I'm unclassifiable. I don't need you to verify this. I see it for myself. I alone am the authority on what I am here because I alone am here.

Waking up to your True Self is being born into a new life. You are no longer imprisoned in your appearance.

This is the source of great freedom,

confidence, wonder, joy, love, peace…

Self-Portrait

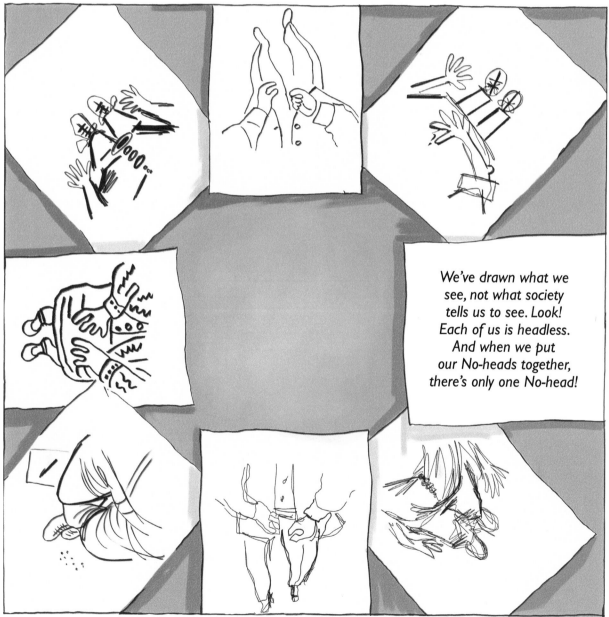

The No-Head Circle

Look down at the circle of bodies.

No dividing lines at the top.

Many bodies hanging out of one Space!

I've grown lots of legs!

Many voices in one Silence!

I am you.

Down there we are many, at the top we are One.

The Sun Of My Soul

Between your arms is your unique view out.

Your view out overlaps with the views out of others.

You experience only your view out. You hear about the other views out.

You are looking at your view out from this boundless Consciousness.

We experience one of the views from this Consciousness and hear about the others.

Many views from One Consciousness!

This is a way of thinking about the mystery of the One that is Many.

Consciousness is like the sun. One Light, many rays.

Douglas gathered together in the *Toolkit* the growing number of experiments.

TOOLKIT FOR TESTING THE INCREDIBLE HYPOTHESIS

He made one hundred copies and gave them away.

HYPOTHESIS
'Closer is He than breathing and nearer than hands and feet.'

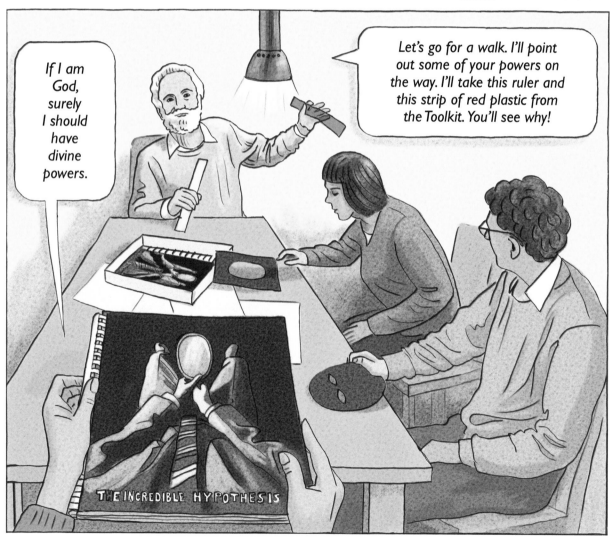

If I am God, surely I should have divine powers.

Let's go for a walk. I'll point out some of your powers on the way. I'll take this ruler and this strip of red plastic from the Toolkit. You'll see why!

THE INCREDIBLE HYPOTHESIS

Dropping all preconceptions, look at yourself as if for the first time and, childlike, trust what you find.

When I close and open my eyes, for you the world doesn't change. What happens when **you** do that?

I destroy and re-create the world!

That's one of your divine powers. You have others.

You see me walking whilst the world remains still.

And I make everything move!

You see me shrink to fit through this gate.

But the gate expands to accommodate me!

Now it's smaller again.

You have the power to make things grow and shrink.

An owl! When I look at it I make it the centre of the world.

I see what you mean.

Whatever you look at, you honour it by promoting it to the centre, like a king honouring a subject in his court by bringing her forward, in front of everyone else.

I look down at my body.

Now I look up at the sky. All the while I remain visible to you.

When I look up, I disappear!

Now I re-appear!

Appearing and disappearing. Magic!

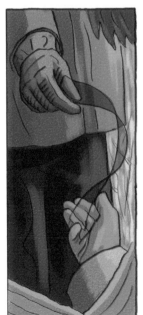

How do my powers benefit me?

They don't bring outward benefits, but inwardly they confirm your divine status.

The One within me is great!

You are a wonder. **The** Wonder. How powerful you are! What imagination and creative flair!

And not only are you creating each thing, you are also creating yourself.

You are God mysteriously conjuring yourself out of nothing!

Self-origination! This is the greatest magic of all!

Douglas distilled personal development into four stages.

1. As a baby you're headless – space for the world.

You're not the one in the mirror.

You are unaware that others see you as a baby.

2. As a child you're learning to be the one in the mirror.

That's Douglas.

That's you.

'Putting on your face.'

Imagine this – grab your face in the mirror,

pull it out,

flip it inside-out,

stretch it to fit

and put it on.

PLOP

Now you think of yourself as others see you.

Well done, Douglas.

But often, as a child, you forget to wear your face.

3. As an adult you wear your face all day.

That's me.

You've shrunk from being everything to a tiny part.

No surprise if you feel insecure, imprisoned, alienated…

4. The seer.

Now I live a two-sided life. Publicly I'm a person, privately I'm capacity for the world.

What a relief! Inner safety, freedom, reunion with the world.

Some of Douglas' young friends had taken LSD.

Douglas, do you want to take a trip?

I'd like to experience it.

One evening.

One each! It will last all night.

The Silence seems even deeper than usual.

Let's do an experiment.

You became the frightening goblin in the coal-cellar from my childhood!

In the morning.

I'm glad I experienced it, but I won't do it again.

It was a peak experience that passed. One's True Self is a 'valley' experience — humble, yes, but always here, always reliable.

Douglas was firing on all cylinders. He wrote more books and continued travelling.

ME

The Science of the 1st PERSON

THE HIDDEN GOSPEL

THE HIDDEN G

GAMES FOR THE KINGDOM

Holland | Canada

Belgium | France

Switzerland | USA

Answer this Zen koan: "How can you swallow the whole of the West River in one gulp?"

New York

The West River isn't nearby but the East River is. Stand by it facing upriver. Watch it flow into your Wide Mouth!

He wrote articles.

THE MIDDLE WAY
JOURNAL OF THE BUDDHIST SOCIETY

The Mountain Path

A Buddhist Workshop

Perseus and the Gorgon

Douglas continued teaching comparative religion.

He had visitors most weekends and often in the week.

1975. BBC 2: The Inside Story.

Douglas, we start filming in ten minutes.

Your energy and creativity are boundless!

I rely on the Source – "the well that never runs dry".

127

Do not delude yourself. No one here will become Enlightened in this life.

That's directed at me! I've been coming for 17 years but this is the last time.

Beryl agreed we could use both houses for this ten-day gathering whilst she's away.

Instead of testing our experience by Jesus' words, we'll test his words by our experience.

THE HIDDEN GOSPEL

"Where two or three are gathered together in My name, there I AM in the midst of them."

Yes. This Space that our bodies emerge from is the I AM that Jesus spoke about – in our midst.

"Jesus said: Take, eat, this is my body."

VOID

This food disappears into the One. Matter becomes spirit. Every meal is Holy Communion!

When Beryl returned ...

Douglas, our relationship has died. I'm leaving.

You have this house. I'll live in the other one.

No, I'm moving to Ipswich.

I'm starting a newsletter for our growing community.

I've designed a logo for it, Anne.

Richard, you're the first person to read the whole of the big version of The Hierarchy.

It's an astonishing book, Douglas. The world should know about it!

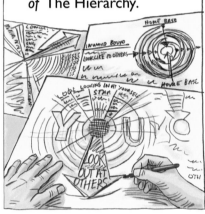
I could make a model of The Hierarchy.

The Youniverse Explorer is a model of each of us.

On the outsides are the layers of your body. On the insides are the layers of your mind.

Start recording the audio guide, Douglas.

I designed The Youniverse Explorer to help me pose this most exciting of questions: What am I?

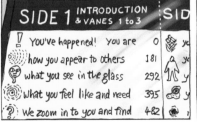
A GUIDE FOR COSMONAUTS

SIDE 1 INTRODUCTION & VANES 1 to 3

You've happened! You are 0
how you appear to others 181
what you see in the glass 292
what you feel like and need 395
We zoom in to you and find 482

A letter from Hal in the Carter Administration.

Director of Education for the Gifted and Talented

August 31, 1976

I congratulate you for your incredible creativity. This is the most exciting and low-cost curriculum aid I have ever seen!

Why is the Director of Education in America interested in The Youniverse Explorer?

Hal recognises it's a much-needed model of the total field of knowledge.

It places every subject studied at school within an organic whole.

Not only that, each layer is a layer of you, an appearance of your Centre.

If a subject is not relevant to us, it's hard to stay interested.

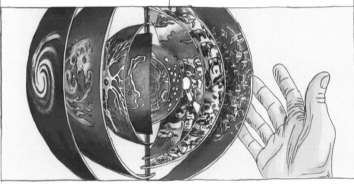

But in one glance students see that each subject is relevant because they are learning about a layer of themselves.

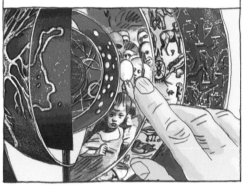

Biology, chemistry and physics study the closer layers of oneself,

history, politics, literature… the middle layers,

geology, geography, astronomy… the outer layers.

Now a student can say, "School is about me!"

Every school should have one!

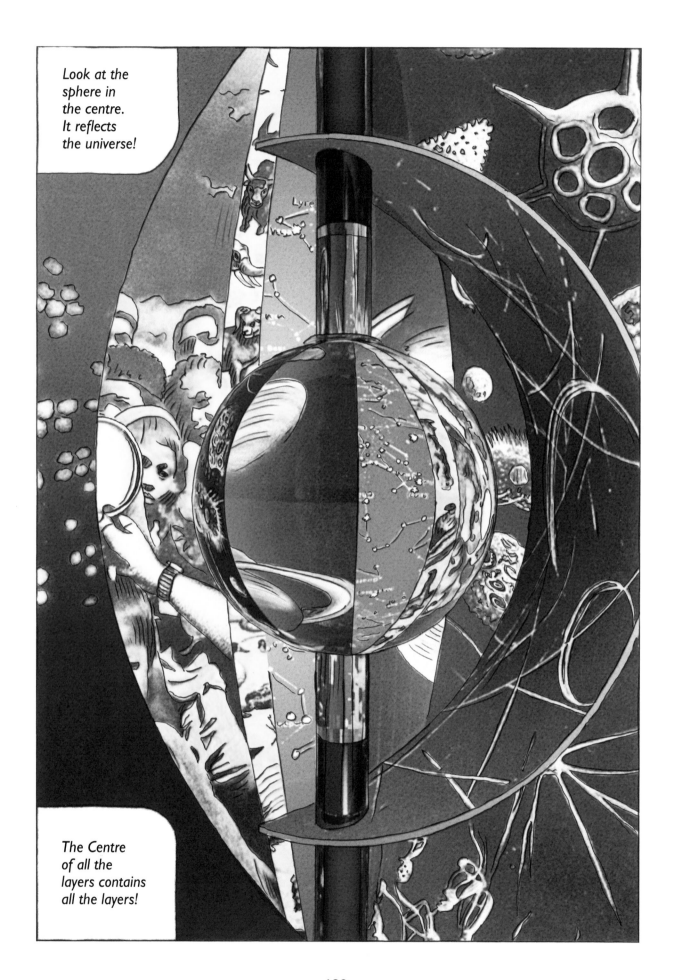

Look at the
sphere in
the centre.
It reflects
the universe!

The Centre
of all the
layers contains
all the layers!

Douglas wrote a story, an odyssey through the Youniverse's layers.

('G. N. Idrah' is 'Harding' backwards.)

I'm Youlysses. For the first time ever I hear a sound in the endless silence. A song. Who is singing? I want to know.

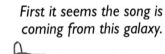

First it seems the song is coming from this galaxy.

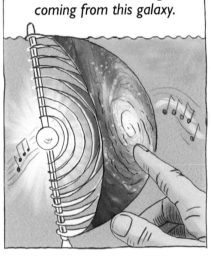

Suddenly the Wormwolf appears. He starts chasing me.

I escape by jumping into the galaxy. I discover a star. Is this the singer?

But the Wormwolf keeps pursuing me.

Jumping into the star to escape, I find a planet – Earth. This must be the singer! I want to rest here but the Wormwolf won't let me stop. He hounds me again.

133

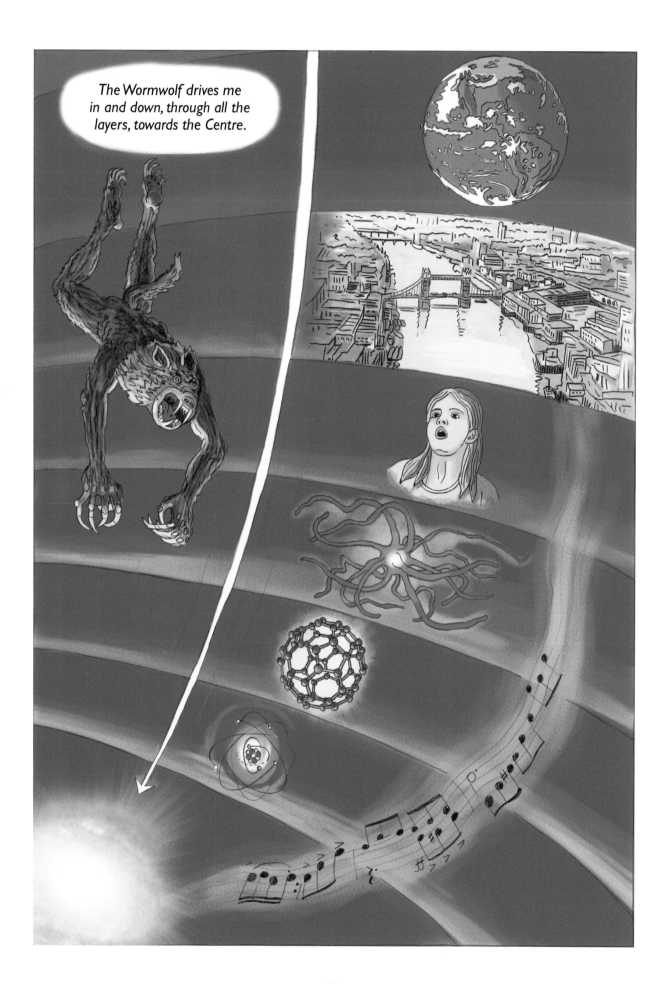

Chased all the way into the Centre, I become nothing.

At last I discover where the song is coming from.

Emptiness! Silence!

Turning round and looking out, I find everything comes from here!

Because the Wormwolf would not let me stop before the Centre, he is really my friend.

He is life's difficulties that keep pushing me home to my True Self.

Douglas rented out Under Shollond.

Here are the keys.

I'm a failure and a fraud. I don't walk my talk. I'm Big Mouth Douglas!

I'm unworthy of the trust God has put in me to do the job of sharing Seeing.

Anne, I'm hardly sleeping.

He's talking a lot, is euphoric then depressed, is making crazy drawings.

I feel abandoned by man and God.

The pipe from the well to the house is blocked.

Like my connection to the Source.

I'm being made to feel my nothingness in my bones.

After three weeks.

Is this crisis over, Douglas?

Yes, Anne, though I still feel unworthy.

But I'm more convinced now of the mercy of God, that He accepts me with all my faults.

Surrendering to God's will is the heart of the matter.

Werner Erhard wants to meet in London.

Who is he?

He's the influential American founder of est — Erhard Seminars Training.

Douglas, I am truly excited about your work. I want to put you on tour.

As long as I'm free to do my thing.

I'd like to do the next training in London, so I understand est better.

I'll arrange it.

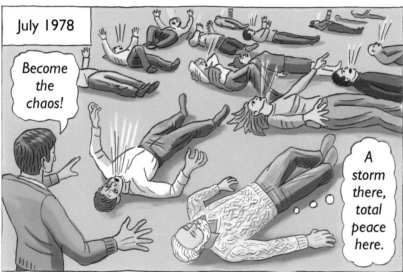

July 1978

Become the chaos!

A storm there, total peace here.

1979. est presented Douglas in eight U.S. cities.

The est Foundation presents: "The Headless Way"

An Evening with Douglas Harding

San Diego, Seattle, Honolulu, Denver, Aspen, Houston, Chicago, Philadelphia

The Yellow Toolkit, designed by Douglas, was given to each participant.

peeling the onion

YOU

Denver

Douglas is one of the first Western philosophers to say that Enlightenment is instantaneous.

Two thousand people and I don't feel under inspection!

Back in England.

Hardly anyone has contacted you from the tour.

It's disappointing, but Seeing doesn't hold on to people.

Anyway it's not a numbers game. After all, there's only One.

Stages Of The Way

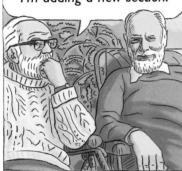

My book On Having No Head *is being re-published. I'm adding a new section.*

For a time, after first Seeing, the benefits can be obvious.

DETACHMENT
JOY
PEACE

But after perhaps years of practice you realise you are clinging like ivy to your separative self.

Was all my progress fraudulent?

You've come to the Barrier — the ego's resistance to the Self.

Discouraged, you may give up on Seeing…

or you go into the Dark Night.

The way through the Darkness involves surrendering your personal will.

141

Letting go of your separate self,

you are reborn each day at Centre as the divine I AM.

The profound surrender of your personal will leads to the Breakthrough.

Now **passively** accepting the present moment becomes **actively** willing it.

Now you say 'yes', unconditionally, to whatever happens.

Profound Declaration of Intent: My desire is that all shall be as it is since all flows from my True Nature.

Douglas continued writing.

I'm 77. I'm getting closer to death.

St. Paul asks: "O Death, **where** is your sting? O Grave, **where** is your victory?"

I reply, "**There,** about two feet away,

not **here** at zero inches!"

The heart of my message is non-verbal.

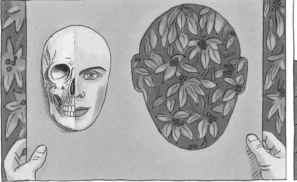

The literature on dying will never be the same again.
Ram Dass

D.E. HARDING
THE LITTLE BOOK OF LIFE AND DEATH
FOREWORD BY RAM DASS

Write about stress, Douglas. Everyone is talking about it.

Through you the Source has given me my next job!

STRESS

Cease overlooking the stress-free Centre you're living from.

The long-time effect of Seeing on my stressfulness is profound. Stressful circumstances have ceased to be anything of the sort.

D.E. HARDING
HEAD OFF STRESS
Beyond the bottom line

1988. Douglas' relationship with Anne changed.

I'm profoundly grateful for everything, Douglas,

but I need space to explore and work things out on my own from now on.

I understand, Anne. You must go your own way.

143

Douglas wrote a courtroom drama.

You are charged with the capital offence of blasphemy.

Our 27 witnesses have confirmed you are human, not divine.

We can all see you are a man in this courtroom.

That's because you are looking at **me**.

If you look at **yourselves** you'll see what I see.

I am not a man and I am not in this courtroom, it is in me: in this One Consciousness that lights up the world.

I am this Light. Here is no spark of that Fire but the blazing Furnace itself, alone and eternal.

Tell that to the executioner, blasphemer!

The jury will retire to reach their verdict.

Do what you like to me, I will live from what I see is here, not from what you say is here. And I will tell the world about it.

D.E. HARDING

THE TRIAL OF THE MAN WHO SAID HE WAS GOD

This book so engages the mind that the heart sings.

Father Gerard Hughes

1991

Douglas, you're 82, you've been travelling for two months yet you have tons of energy!

Because I don't go anywhere.

I didn't come to Australia, Australia came to me!

I hear you're writing another book.

Yes. The Spectre In The Lake. *It's a modern Pilgrim's Progress.*

The hero expands to become everything, but then succumbs to pride.

A crisis follows.

He's put in a mental hospital to 'normalise' him, to cut him down to size.

The hero's redemption involves going through a door into the dark catacombs of a castle...

After a perilous journey he is reborn.

Now he has greater respect for his human self, 'the spectre in the lake',

as well as his divine Self.

It's the story of my life!

It's also a love story.

As I grow older I realise more profoundly that love is what it's all about.

As he was finishing this book, Douglas fell in love.

Paris. May, 1991

Catherine, come to the Douglas Harding workshop.

I'm not interested in gurus!

He's not a guru. I'm taking you there!

Are you looking out of two eyes or one boundless Space?

At last, someone who is making available the **experience** of the Self.

Your experiments are fantastic. They work.

I see you've got the message! Let's stay in touch.

February, 1992. Douglas was in France again.

Catherine, my translator has let me down. Can you step in?

D'accord!

Qui êtes-vous vraiment?

JE SUIS TOUT
JE SUIS HUMAIN +
JE SUIS

You translated brilliantly.

It feels natural. Two voices, one Consciousness!

I'm back in France in August. Will you help me again?

I'd love to.

October 1992

My home is your home.

My ship has found its harbour.

146

Catherine and Douglas travelled often, giving many workshops together – America, Israel, Japan, France… They married in February, 1995.

Meeting Catherine has made a big difference in your life, Douglas.

Yes. To live more fully one needs a companion. I'm continually learning from Catherine.

We don't always agree.

Catherine has her own point of view. But this ding-dong, this debate, is good for both of us.

If I feel irritated by Douglas, I come back here and am Space for him. Then my irritation dissolves and there's no real problem.

In love with Catherine, Douglas' heart opened more.

The advent of Catherine in my life is a godsend, a miracle.

We walk hand in hand, looking in the same direction.

Out at the world and in at the Source.

Having both a male and a female voice in a workshop is a good balance.

I preach, Catherine charms!

Video Interview, 2001

What is your work about, Douglas?

Seeing that you are not what you look like, Richard!

The experiments are crucial

because they make who we really are accessible to all.

Society doesn't recognise this new science, the science of the 1st Person.

Astonishing, isn't it! But the truth will prevail.

My maps, and The Youniverse Explorer model, are also important.

They also point to the One.

Is this therapy? What about the mind?

Where is your mind?

My thoughts and feelings are not in a container here, separate from the world.

My mind is at large.

Seeing heals the imagined split between the self and the world.

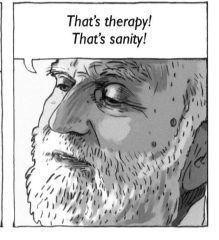

That's therapy! That's sanity!

After twenty years alone with Seeing, you now have many friends.

It's a blessing to share this with others.

This Clarity is the only thing you can be sure of sharing.

What I see as blue might be your red, but here at Centre there's nothing to differ about.

This nothingness isn't just nothing, is it?

149

No. It's also everything. And it's awake!

At your heart is the Kingdom, the Power and the Glory!

It's the most obvious thing in the world. It's begging to be noticed!

What about trust?

Seeing who you really are without trusting it is no good really.

The whole practical business of life involves shifting trust from what you look like to what you are,

from that pinhead in the mirror to this Immensity at your Centre.

You probably won't get what you want, but you will get what you really need.

If we can't trust this, what can we trust? The know-how at our Centre is fabulous!

150

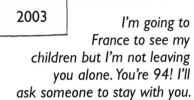
2003

I'm going to France to see my children but I'm not leaving you alone. You're 94! I'll ask someone to stay with you.

No! I'll be fine, Catherine. Go!

You're stubborn!

The phone!

DRRRING.....
DRRRING....

DING DONG

The doorbell rang.

The door's open. Come in, I need help!

We'll call an ambulance.

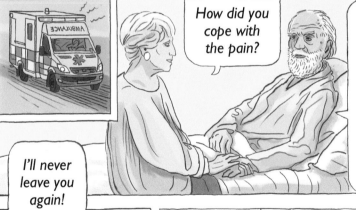
How did you cope with the pain?

I couldn't surrender to the pain, but I surrendered to my inability to surrender!

My rescuers were Jehovah's Witnesses. I was saved by Jehovah's Witnesses!

I'll never leave you again!

You've grown wheels!

Yes.

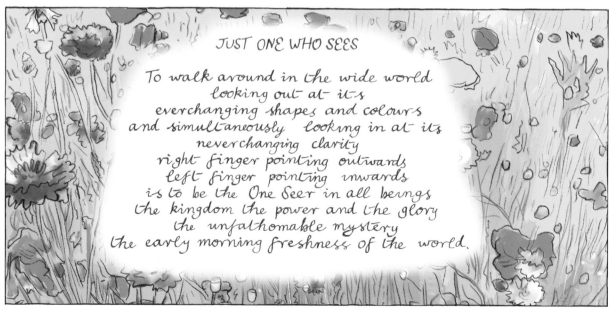

Occasionally Douglas saw his children.

Hello, Father.

Lydia!

Simon! Julian!

December 2006

Douglas caught pneumonia.

I'm here with you, Douglas.

You seem to drift in and out of consciousness, Douglas.

It's very interesting to die, David. Change there, no change here.

Yes, Richard.

We will make sure this beautiful, simple, direct way Home flourishes in the world, Douglas.

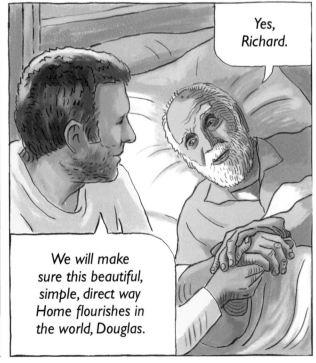

He's pointing at his father.

Yes, Colin. He loved him dearly.

I don't want you to die, Douglas.

You must let me go now, Catherine. I'm going home.

January 11, 2007

Catherine, wake up. Douglas is no longer breathing.

He's gone home.

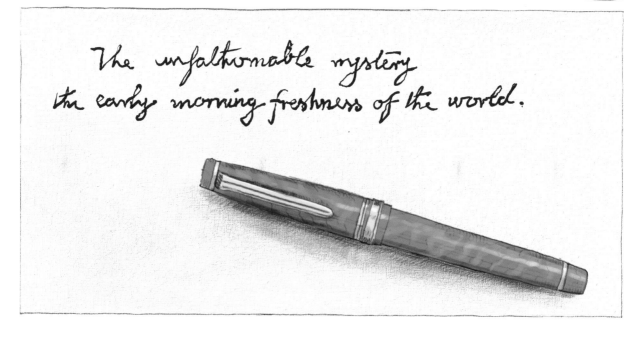

The unfathomable mystery
the early morning freshness of the world.

THE KINGDOM OF HEAVEN
IS WITHIN YOU

DOUGLAS
EDISON
HARDING
1909-2007
Beloved husband of
CATHERINE

THE·KINGDOM·OF·HEAVEN
IS·WITHIN·YOU

On Creating This Book

In 2012 I made a film about the life and ideas of Douglas Harding and published it on YouTube. Victor Lunn-Rockliffe is an artist I had corresponded with for several years. He saw the film and suggested it would make a good graphic biography. We exchanged emails exploring the idea – I didn't even know what a graphic biography was, never mind how you create one! But it sounded like a thrilling idea, so I said 'yes'.

My task was to write the script. I would email my ideas to Victor about each page. Victor would then make a rough sketch which was followed by a detailed drawing and then the full-colour version. It was fascinating to see each page materialise, appearing magically out of nothing! We conducted the whole process via the internet. In fact it wasn't until the summer of 2015 that I met Victor. Before then we hadn't even spoken on the phone! All I can say in our defence is that we live in different parts of the world – I live in north-east London and Victor lives in west London...

My part of the project involved researching Douglas' life, drawing not only on the many conversations I had with him – we were friends for more than 35 years – but also on interviews conducted with him and conversations I had with friends who knew him. I also have in my possession many of his papers, letters, diaries and notebooks as well as many photographs of Douglas, photographs of people who featured in his life, and photographs of places where he lived. We have drawn on all of these resources to create a picture of Douglas' life and the development of his ideas as faithfully as we could.

On behalf of Victor and myself I would like to thank the friends who have read and re-read our various drafts and made so many helpful, inspiring comments.

In 1996 I set up The Shollond Trust, a UK charity whose aim is to help make more widely available Douglas Harding's philosophy. You can access more resources about the Headless Way on the Trust's website – headless.org

Richard Lang

Books by Douglas Harding

Almost all the books by Douglas Harding listed below are available via the shop on the Headless Way website (headless.org).

Short Stories
The Meaning and Beauty of the Artificial
How Briggs Died
The Melwold Mystery
An Unconventional Portrait of Yourself
The Hierarchy of Heaven and Earth
Visible Gods
On Having No Head
Religions of the World
The Face Game
The Science of the 1st Person
The Hidden Gospel
Journey to the Centre of the Youniverse
The Little Book of Life and Death
Head Off Stress
The Trial of the Man who said he was God
Look For Yourself
The Spectre in the Lake
To Be And Not To Be
The Turning Point
Just One Who Sees
As I See It

Other Publications

Face to No-Face (David Lang)
Seeing Who You Really Are (Richard Lang)
Open to the Source (Richard Lang)
A Flower in the Desert (David Lang)
The Light that I am (J.C. Amberchele)
Celebrating Who We Are (Richard Lang)
Incredible Countries (Colin Oliver)
The Freedom to Love (Karin Visser)
The Youniverse Explorer (while stocks last)
Videos of Douglas Harding are available via the website.